APRIL

S	1	8	15	22	29
M	2	9	16	23	30
Tu	3	10	17	24	—
W	4	11	18	25	—
Th	5	12	19	26	—
F	6	13	20	27	—
S	7	14	21	28	—

D0276615

Tu	1	8	15	22	29
W	2	9	16	23	30
Th	3	10	17	24	31
F	4	11	18	25	—
S	5	12	19	26	—

JUNE

S	—	3	10	17	24
M	—	4	11	18	25
Tu	—	5	12	19	26
W	—	6	13	20	27
Th	—	7	14	21	28
F	1	8	15	22	29
S	2	9	16	23	30

CONTENTS

The
Fireside Book

A picture and a poem
for every mood
chosen by

David Hope

Printed and published by
D.C. THOMSON & CO., LTD.,
185 Fleet Street, LONDON EC4A 2HS.
© D.C. Thomson & Co., Ltd., 2006
ISBN 1-84535-158-4

WINTER SPIRIT

I AM the cold on frosty days
  That makes your noses glow,
I turn the trees to sugar sticks
And bring the flakes of snow.
I am a robin on a fence
With breast of scarlet red,
I make the stars a tapestry
When children are in bed.

I am a scene of pure delight
When snowflakes clothe the land,
The hills are sugar dumplings
I made with tender hand.
I am a sky of Winter blue
With wisps of lacy cloud,
I give the sun a gentle face
That does not call aloud.

Peter Cardwell

NOT WASTED TIME

NOT wasted time this February day
To sit and look in sun poured out
Unstinting from a cup so Summer full
And warm. To sit and look
At velvet beech trunks, smoky-grey,
Their branches reaching up to stroke the sky
With splayed and sprayed-out twigs
So intricate and interlaced . . .
Not wasted time this February day
To sit and be alive.

Alice Elder

SPRINGTIME STAKES

IT'S time to start the Springtime Stakes,
as eagerly each one partakes,
Jostling at the starting gate,
over is the dormant wait.
The flag is up, the race begun,
a true and steadfast course they'll run,
To set our flagging hearts aglow
the snowdrop is the first to show.
The going's soft with gentle rain,
her little flowers to sustain,
Then o'er the hill in hot pursuit,
stretching gentle stem and root,
Comes the primrose at a pace,
so happily to find her place.
(I'm sure that, if she only could,
she'd take a shortcut thro' the wood!)
Close on their heels and going fast,
the vivid crocus comes at last,
Her striking colours, hues and tints,
shining as the sunlight glints.
Whilst dandelion and buttercup
in the paddock limber up,
But, when all is said and done,
no matter who we think has won,
For long before the racing starts,
each one of them has won our hearts!

Brian H. Gent

GEESE

WITH sudden clatter
   they rise from the stubble,
wings beating
in noisy flight;
to quickly return
cackling loudly
in a long drawn-out line,
swerving from side to side,
then they bunch,
drop, dive bomb in,
spread out again,
search the ground
like aeroplanes
ready to attack.

Landing in platoons,
they skid across hoar frost,
pierce the scattered potatoes
left lying to break
their long Winter hunger.

Ruth M. L. Walker

WILD GARLIC

ALL through the Winter the rain beat down
  And churned the woodland floor to
mud and sludge.
The drier Spring peeled off the slime
But still left surface dismal brown
Until one April week, another flood —
Of green — flowed in.

But then, in May, as though to make amends,
The green was spiked with constellations
Of the sharpest white: wild garlic
Shining on that woodland floor
Inverted to a canopy of stars.

Alice Elder

FAIRIES

I'M sure there must be fairies
down by the potting shed,
And in between the rockery
and round the flower bed.
Although I've never seen them
I'm sure they must be there,
For last night, when I went to bed,
the ground was bleak and bare.
But then, whilst I was sleeping,
they must have cast their spell,
Because I woke this morning
to see snowdrops in the dell.

Brian H. Gent

WHEN . . .

WHEN golden sun-shafts split the sky,
And clouds of birds go raining by;
When bearded boughs are shaven clean,
And buds of hawthorn lather green;
When streamlets flow like liquid glass,
And lambs bob up in seas of grass;
When dawn breaks out — a rash of light —
And feverish larks infect the night;
When drops of fresh-brewed water fall,
And thirsty meadows drink them all;
When Life wakes, wide-eyed, after rest,
Of all the seasons — that's the best!

Glynfab John

THE SINNER

TORN-eared Tom, the cat next door,
   Has some habits I deplore.
He caught a mouse the other day,
And waltzed in with it, just to say:
"I won't do this for everyone;
A drop of milk and I'll be gone."

Torn-eared Tom in depths of night
Prowls the gardens full of fight:
Spit and snarl and screech and curse,
Flying fur and even worse.
Then home he comes when daylight dawns,
Licks a paw and widely yawns.

Tom can scratch and Tom can bite,
He puts the other cats to flight.
He's just a thug, a ne'er-do-well,
And how he'll end up who can tell.
Down our way it's understood
He's feline boss of the neighbourhood.

His owner is a lady fair
Who thinks her cat's beyond compare.
She buys him fish and tins of meat,
And murmurs softly, "Aren't you sweet!"
But Tom upon her lap just grins,
Unrepentant of his sins.

Peter Cliffe

UMBRELLAS

UMBRELLAS — all shapes and all sizes
  Have sprouted as mushrooms might grow,
Or that's how it looks from my window
When watching the street far below.
Just moments ago there was promise
Of sunshine deliciously warm,
Then clouds seemed to gather from nowhere,
And suddenly — crash! — what a storm.
And that's when the brollies came shooting
Like fungi, all dappled with light,
So though, down below, rain is falling,
From here, every prospect looks bright!

Margaret Ingall

TWO GOLDFINCHES

TWO of them came to the table
   Dressed in their finery
Of feathered gilt,
Showing off their wealth
Of crimson, black,
Vestal white, dark brown,
Bars of gold about their wings.

The blue tits returned
To find their status demoted,
Suddenly looking more like pages
In tight-fitting sailor-boy uniforms,
Watching the happy couple
Take a wedding feast,
And looking bereaved, bereft.

David Elder

SPRING MORNING

THE morning dawned wide-eyed and flushed with rose,
To dance barefoot upon the early dew.
She kissed the crocus buds to wakefulness
And filled the dreaming woods with endless blue.

Her wind-songs lent their magic to the day,
As blithely down the verdant hills she came,
To spangle every eager tree with leaf
And touch the chestnut candles into flame.

Joan Howes

LARK OR OWL?

ARE you a lark or are you an owl?
  Do you leap from your bed, or creep with a scowl?
Do you love the new morn, and walk with a spring,
Or dream of the dusk when the nightingales sing?
Do you buzz like a bee when the sun's shining bright,
Or glow like a star in the moon's silver light?
Whatever your nature, whatever your views
You'll find a reward in whatever you choose,
For though she keeps turning as hours move by,
The world has a beauty to please every eye.

Margaret Ingall

THE TRANQUIL HOUR . . .

HERE, primrose constellations glow
Protected by the foxglove spire;
There, tulips trimmed with sparkling dew;
Laburnums pooling shades of fire.
Where cuckoo flutes his timeless call,
Re-echoed over hill and dale,
The silken drapes of blossoms fall
To spread a pastel cloak and veil.
Where dappled sunshine smoothly spills
In filtered rays of dazzling light,
To keen the note of lark on wing
As up and up, it soars in flight . . .

Elizabeth Gozney

FRAGMENTS
— MAYTIME

BRIGHT as a Van Gogh
the buttercup field
is a masterpiece
of Spring's bravura.

Bluebells in clay woods
welcome space-walkers
leaving no place
for the rambler's foot.

Clover's clapper
sways like a metronome
on a keyboard vamped
by a windswept busker.

Pristine white
the hawthorn stoops
to show off sleeves
full of surprises.

Robust and muscly
cow parsley provides
an ample shoulder
for roads to lean on.

Wild briar prepares
for hedgerow quarrels
as new fern claws
threateningly uncurl.

John Ellis

A CHARMING PLACE

WALK by a stream when darkness halts
  The birds' endearing prayer;
Where fragrance of the woodbine seeps
Into the cooling air;
Where little dizzy insects play,
And moths, in graceful glide,
Amuse themselves whilst Phoebe bathes
Her face in sparkling tide.

Sit on the banks, adorned with moss,
Thick-growing year by year.
Listen to sighing winds, and sense
The magic atmosphere:
Then, if tomorrow brings you gloom,
Recall this charming place,
Tranquil as Mother Nature planned,
Unspoiled by human race.

Alice Jean Don

NIGHT-IMAGERY

THE sabre-moon, unsheathed
from its scabbard of white
cloud, glints and penetrates
with a tempered-steel light,
slashing at the backcloth
of a purple-draped sky,
while bright chariot-stars
through the universe fly.

In deep forests of sleep,
dream-haunted, slumber-dim,
gallons of ghostliness
overflow the mind's brim,
and, lining the lakeside's
darkness-pleated skirt-edge,
creatures dart, protected
by sharp sentries of sedge.

Glynfab John

SWALLOWS

ONE day when Spring has come again to green the trees
And in the fields the flowers bend and blow
The swallows swim the air, they play the breeze,
Returned three thousand miles across the flow
And swell of tides, the moiling of the seas.
And no-one's ever found, and no-one knows,
What strength it is that brings them back to free
Their flight above our lives, our serried rows
Of terraced worlds and ordered days of ease.
Yet now the west winds change, the old earth tilts
A fraction in her chains, the light goes grey
So through the wood a chase of bright leaves spins.
The dark begins to grow, the Autumn wilts
And every dusk the swallows flit and play,
Their sojourn all but done, their time here in.
We stare at Winter windows all day long
Watching where they were, knowing they are gone.

Kenneth C. Steven

SEASONAL VIEWS

IN hedgerow seek the primrose bud,
  Its curling heart unfold;
While daffodils' swathed trumpets flow
A tossed bouquet of gold.
Watch bluebells shimmer in a sea
Of waving, misty plumes,
And fleeting showers, lightly skim
On hawthorn's cream-laced blooms.
Each season brings its special charm,
Its colours rainbow bright,
To blend within a spectrum's view
Of ever changing light . . .

Elizabeth Gozney

A MAGIC NIGHT

GIVE me a fine night's pleasantries —
The moonlight dancing through the trees;
Serenity of sleeping hills;
Clear tinkling of the hidden rills.
A night when leafy woodlands calm
Release a copious dew-laced balm.
A gentle night that's sure to bring
The tawny owl on silent wing.

Give me a night when soft winds glow,
Caressing rivers in their flow,
And whispering to birds cocooned
Among the scented bine festooned;
When every quiet moonlit trail
Seems borrowed from a fairytale;
When valleys lie in perfect bliss —
A magic night, oh give me this.

Alice Jean Don

RUMBLING BRIDGE

ONE Summer afternoon you go
   Up the silvering of the river, low
Under the green cathedral of the leaves
Lemoned by sunlight, the slow wheel of gold
High in the huge sky.
Up there, above the flutes of the falls
You lower yourself into the delicious gasp of river,
Rock downwards through stone gullies,
Fleeces of water, deep runnels, curls and eddies,
Smoothings the colour of whisky.
You stay water-tobogganing the whole day long until the sun
Has bled to death behind the hills,
Till the wind whispers in the trees, shudders them,
And everything is only different shades of blue.
You trail home with sandshoes
As a slip of moon lifts over the pine trees
And the bats weave their own mime through June air.
You come home and stand
And don't want to go inside,
Don't want to close your door on this day
Till the last of the light is lost.

Kenneth C. Steven

TO JANE

THE keen stars were twinkling,
   And the fair moon was rising among them,
Dear Jane.
The guitar was tinkling,
But the notes were not sweet till you sung them
Again.

As the moon's soft splendour
O'er the faint cold starlight of Heaven
Is thrown,
So your voice most tender
To the strings without soul had then given
Its own.

The stars will awaken,
Though the moon sleeps a full hour later
Tonight;
No leaf will be shaken
Whilst the dews of your melody scatter
Delight.

Though the sound overpowers,
Sing again, with your dear voice revealing
A tone
Of some world far from ours,
Where music and moonlight and feeling
Are one.

Percy Bysshe Shelley

ENCROACHMENT

THE squirrel sliding down my scullery wall
Frightening feeding birds with bold impunity.
The field mouse waiting for their scraps to fall.
The hedgehog snuffling in the tidied leaves
Warned me
Of the forest far beyond my fence
Awaiting opportunity.

If the wood returns once more
To make of my hard-won bower a mockery
Will I hear in the night the quiet snore
Of the great bear sleeping in the compost heap
See once again
The grey wolf in the moonlight
Standlng
On the rockery?

Ian Olson

THE OLD COVERED BRIDGE

HOW well I remember! How could I forget
Those warm, sunny evenings, the place where we met?
It was mentioned with laughter, and sometimes a frown,
The old covered bridge on the edge of the town.

It was there I first kissed you, well hidden within,
A funny old place for romance to begin;
Astride Christmas Creek, where the water runs brown,
The old covered bridge on the edge of the town.

We're no longer young, but the bridge is still there,
Unpainted and tottering, holes everywhere.
One day it will stagger, come tumbling down,
The old covered bridge on the edge of the town.

Peter Cliffe

HERON

THIS long-legged bird,
   stands motionless
as a shroud,
partially submerged
in the sluggish current.

Long after the wailing gulls
have ceased their chatter,
it maintains its vigil
in the darkening light,
neck held erect,
spear beak ready
to pounce.

Then it pierces the water,
transfixing the trout
at a glance, raises
its throat, then,
with hoarse, croaking cry,
flies off to its
tree-top nest.

Ruth M. L. Walker

BUDDLEIA

YOU have your share of visitors
  In Summer, purple princess,
Your high and honeyed fragrance
Beckoning from afar.
Bees and butterflies, early in the day
Busying and fluttering
Beneath the morning star.
Tortoiseshell and peacock,
Languid black-tipped whites,
And a pretty painted lady
Who journeyed through the night.
Those dark and frail fritillaries,
And fractious hover flies,
A skipper and a swallowtail
With wings that mesmerise.
But now the days are drawing in,
Your prominence grown brown,
And we must wait until next year
For a newly-fashioned crown.

Don Robinson

DOLGOCH FALLS

SLIP-SLIDING, side-stepping,
  sheer-faced and fell-falling,
flash and slap and flurry,
tear-laced whitewater flume,
booming and dinning and spuming,
bending on boulder and scar
and crag, skiing magnificent
silver-sheen-thin down over
green-glazed mazes of rock,
alternately broken and raucous;
cascading cool and unruly
and white as moonshine into
occasional glaucous lagoons,
soft-spoken-smooth, pleasingly
clear and hyaline, soothingly,
teasingly pier-glass-still;
out again dashingly, crashing
downhill, swimmingly, seemingly
breathless and brash, spilled
over and gone, enslaved to flow
and race and splash; ensnared yet
never stilled or jading in this
jade place its passage engraved:
hurrying on, yet forever here.

John Ellis

SWIFTS

EACH day they become
Avid readers of the sky,
Skimming the column inches
For items of interest,
Sifting, digesting,
Abstracting insects
That are their staple news,
Sometimes regurgitating
The contents
To hungry offspring,
And sometimes themselves
Making headlines
In the broadsheet
Blue sky.

David Elder

BY THE RIVER

THE river laps the slipway,
The water's calm and still,
The Summer day has scarce begun,
The morning air is chill.
But soon the sun will break the cloud,
The mist will burn away,
The ducks, the town, the tourists too
Will wake to start the day.
Bright boats will chug the waterways,
Small dinghies fill the creeks,
The air will fill with voices,
Distant traffic, seagull shrieks,
And busy feet will come and go,
And children laugh and cry,
and trippers pause to eat an ice
and watch the world go by.
Until at last the twilight's hush
reclaims the busy quay
and leaves the river running soft
towards the boundless sea.

Margaret Ingall

BRANCH-LINE TRAIN

TRAILING smoke above the track,
  While turning wheels went clickety-clack,
Reassuring, that refrain:
Friendly little branch-line train.

Never going very fast,
As farms and fields and woods slipped past;
Two shining rails for this small train,
To take folks out and back again.

Not so many trains a day
Came our village station way.
Station staff would pass the hours
Tending beds of pretty flowers.

One short whistle, doors a-slam,
The train was saying: Here I am!
I still can smell it, if I dream,
That lovely mix of smoke and steam.

Stationmaster, dignified,
Wore his uniform with pride;
Not too proud to smile and say:
Have a very pleasant day.

In this age of too much speed,
Maybe these are what we need.
Branch-line trains were fun, you know,
In the not so long ago.

Peter Cliffe

THE FAIRY

LAST night, while walking on my lawn,
I thought I heard a fairy yawn.
Turning about, to my surprise,
I saw a pair of elfin eyes
peeping out of the undergrowth.
Enchanted, I suppressed my breath
and stooped to gaze upon the sprite,
agleam with an unearthly light.
At once the diminutive wean
quite crossly piped this lecture: "Man,
your heavy footsteps as you tread
disturb the fairyfolk abed.
Good humans, surely I am right,
should also be in bed at night."
I thought of this as sounding fair.
Perhaps I had no business there,
making such a thunderous din,
disturbing that poor minikin.
And so, as quietly as a mouse,
I tip-toed back into the house.

John Ellis

THE DREAMING PLACE

WHEN trapped in city noise and strife,
  When life lacks hope or grace,
I close my eyes and visualise
My special dreaming place.
A place where vibrant meadows spring
From rich and fruitful earth,
Where gold is not just traders' coin,
But stuff of truer worth.
It's buttercup and tansy blooms,
And cowslips reaching high,
A quilt of real and living gold
Beneath an open sky.
And here no discord fills the air,
No screech of cars that pass
Just harmony of bird and bee,
And wind among the grass.
So let the city rumble on,
Its streets are not for me
For somewhere is my dreaming place
And there, one day, I'll be.

Margaret Ingall

THE RUIN

WHEN the last colours of the day
  Have from their burning ebbed away,
About that ruin, cold and lone,
The cricket shrills from stone to stone;
And scattering o'er its darkened green,
Bands of fairies may be seen,
Clattering like grasshoppers, their feet
Dancing a thistledown dance round it:
While the great gold of the mild moon
Tinges their tiny acorn shoon.

Walter De La Mare

NIGHT

NIGHT casts its shadow on the ground;
A lone owl, distant, hoots.
The darkness murmurs, dazed with dreams;
A stray star earthward shoots.
And now, the moon! Above the hill,
Her pale face shyly peeps.
Light breaks so softly, glows the sky;
The world, in silence, sleeps.

Glynfab John

NOCTURNAL INTERPLAY

THE waning moon plays hide and seek,
  With clouds around the mountain peak.
Barn owls swoop to catch their prey,
In golden fields of new-mown hay.
And busy excavating moles,
Make little hillocks digging holes.
Badgers from their setts emerge,
With hedgehogs in the grassy verge.
Bats embark on silent flight,
And disappear into the night.
Such sweet nocturnal interplay,
That lasts until the new-born day.

Brian H. Gent

THE FOUNTAIN

THE fountain in the courtyard
is dancing with the breeze,
its water caught and scattered
like raindrops from the trees.
It's whipped to silver splinters
that whirl in windy sky,
it's twirled in shining streamers,
like ribbons leaping high.
It jumps and spurts and splashes
within its mossy sink,
it runs in little puddles
where blackbirds come to drink.
Its song has many voices,
its tunes have many keys,
the fountain in the courtyard
is dancing with the breeze.

Margaret Ingall

DARK SHADOWS

AFTER the cloud passed
And the sky dropped
No more tears,
A rainbow stretched
From hilltop to sea
And planted gold
Where once grey cloud
Cast dark shadows.

David Elder

SUMMER'S ENDING

LEAVES have spiralled to the ground,
   vivid greens now faded,
With arms outstretched and branches bare
trees are looking jaded.
The woodland floor is carpeted
with leaves of russet red,
That swirl and rustle in the breeze
and swish beneath our tread.
A time has come for quietude,
for resting and repose,
Now hips and hawes are shining
on hedge and briar rose.
So sadly we must say farewell
to our dear special friend,
And thank her for her bounty
which now, alas, must end.
Whilst pale lemon shafts of sunlight
are filtered thro' the mist,
The Autumn and the Summertime
will keep their sacred tryst.

Brian H. Gent

AMONG TREES

HOW I have loved trees;
  Saplings fondled by the breeze,
Poplars etched against the sky
Perfect to my wondering eyes.
I recall a sunlit lake
Where willows curtsied clad in lace,
A childhood swing that skimmed the clouds
In crimson maples tall and proud.
I have wandered deep in thought
Through leafy birches' idle talk
And glow of beech when Summer's done,
Dear friends, every one.

Rachel Wallace-Oberle

SEPTEMBER

THE fields lay white beneath a snow of sun
   And birds were restless underneath, they rose and wheeled
Like silver leaves. The skies were more than blue;
Burnished and beaten with a strange brilliance.
The angels are coming, I thought;
The angels will come in the night
When a huge moon ovals through these bright and
   cloudless skies;
They will come to bind the sheaves
While we are fast asleep.
They will work the fields, their wings tight-folded,
All through the white night of this September,
The moon gliding high like a balloon
Over the glazed harvest of the world;
Nothing moving except the angels and the wind, until the
   task is done
In the warm stillness of the dawn.

Kenneth C. Steven

CHESTNUT TRACES

THRILL and celebration
  As the burnished conkers fall
They linger in long grasses
And round the dry stone wall.
There's magic in the chestnut trees
In bright mahogany traces
The nimble fingers gathering
The gems this season graces.
Mellow Autumn's treasure trail
Scattered clasps of fun
Snapping twigs and tumbling fruit
In copper woodland spun.

Dorothy McGregor

UNHURRIED

AMONG the rows of trees undressed
that blush and cast their garb aside
I wander, reverent and pressed,
by Autumn's pomp on every side.

I love her language rich and deep
that fills my strangely aching heart,
of birds in flight, of rose asleep
of icy rain and mornings dark.

My lonely garden sighs and kneels
beneath the touch of Autumn's hand,
her fingertips brush fading fields
and sleepy hills with colours grand.

Spellbound by her brilliant wiles
splashed against low leaden skies,
we watch, entirely beguiled,
the unhurried world and I.

Rachel Wallace-Oberle

LINES COMPOSED IN A WOOD ON A WINDY DAY

MY soul is awakened, my spirit is soaring
And carried aloft on the wings of the breeze;
For above and around me the wild wind is roaring
Arousing to rapture the earth and the seas.

The long, withered grass in the sunshine is glancing
The bare trees are tossing their branches on high
The dead leaves beneath them are merrily dancing
The white clouds are scudding across the blue sky.

I wish I could see how the ocean is lashing
The foam of its billows to whirlwinds of spray
I wish I could see how its proud waves are dashing
And hear the wild roar of their thunder today.

Anne Brontë

I REMEMBER . . .

THOSE days of oh so long ago,
The sunset with its afterglow,
The outings that gave us a thrill,
I remember still . . .

The friendship that we both forged then,
That time we made our tree-top den,
Fishing by the watermill,
I remember still . . .

Sunlight streaming thro' the trees,
The softness of the gentle breeze,
Bluebell haze and daffodil,
I remember still . . .

Those sunny days when you and me,
Went to the summer house for tea,
Roses on the window-sill,
I remember still . . .

Now time has passed and we are old,
Our friendship has been purest gold,
As magic as a skylark's trill,
Dear to my heart — remembered still . . .

Brian H. Gent

FIREWORKS

THE Autumn days are paint-box bright,
   their palettes rich and bold,
a jewelled mosaic of dancing leaves
of scarlet, green and gold.
It's pyrotechnic magic that
our human skill can't match,
and yet, on cold November nights,
we still, with joy, dispatch
our rainbow-coloured rockets and
our jets of sparkling fire,
we let the conflagration blaze,
and watch the sparks fly higher.
And for a few brief moments,
before the year grows cold,
we scatter bright defiant stars
of scarlet, green and gold.

Margaret Ingall

RAIN

WE listen to it drumming on our slates
   Night and day. Little silver fingertips
That seem to leave a queer, bright-shining plate
On all the world. Our youngest tries to slip
To watch, afraid, the river bounding past
Like some great dog in chase, but has to wait
Inside — hearing instead of just how fast
The bridge was swept away, of how a gate
Was snapped like twigs. We light a fire,
Make tea and toast and listen to the news
As bit by bit the world shrinks to one room.
A strange excitement makes things not feel dire
But full of some wild mystery. We lose
Our fear, thrilled by the danger of our doom.

Kenneth C. Steven

AUTUMN LEAVES

ON this day
   That awoke to the knock
Of the wind
At Summer's closed door,
Leaves tap-danced their joy
On the frosted green paths,
Forgetting the past
That stuck
To the high trees.

Now they are free
To roam wherever they wish,
Dancing and darting,
Until Winter arrives
And Autumn
Leaves.

David Elder

STORM

AN avalanche of wind and snow
   hurls itself across my street,
kicking icy frozen feet,
shrieking bitter frigid blows,
flinging cold that snaps the trees
and traces panes with silvered oaths.

My aspen shudders in the yard,
sparrows cower under eaves;
this Winter storm gives no reprieve —
a hoyden spitting glacial shards
that promises before it leaves
to bury Earth in icy stars.

None venture from their houses warm
to brave the onslaught, dare the fray,
but recklessly I vow to stay
out where cold and snow are born,
for on this wild enchanted day
I have met the wintriest storm.

Rachel Wallace-Oberle

THE MOUNTAIN

SNOWCAPPED the mountain's presence
 Bathed in moonbeam's crystal light,
A silver shadowed etching
Through the vigil of the night.
Its grandeur and remoteness,
And impressive peaks on high,
Bring a solitary enchantment
Stretching up towards the sky.
It's a time to be reflecting
In this quietude of space,
Of the mountain's constant presence,
And its lasting, solid grace.

Elizabeth Gozney

POLNEY LOCH

FIVE below. Not a breath
But blue sky above,

The roofs glittering with crystals of frost,
The branches all furred white.

I crackled up the path to the top of the wood,
Listened to the yaffle of two jays

Flickering away into nowhere.
The pond was an eye with a cataract;

A thin shimmer of ice across it.
I broke off a chunk from the edge,

My fingers aching with cold,
Held it in one hand, crouched and skimmed it.

It caught the sun, became a chink of gold
Singing and spinning away.

And suddenly I was five years old,
Finding the world and putting it all together.

Kenneth C. Steven

CHRISTMAS LIGHTS

WHILE I was out awaiting stars
   deep within the vault of night,
I came upon a boulevard,
a spectacle of Christmas lights.
Each house and post and slender spire
seemed to drift against the dark;
all were wreathed in jewelled attire
and left upon the snow a mark
of faceted and blazing flowers
that put the fairest stars to shame,
and lit the gentle slumbering hours
with kaleidoscoplc flame.
I'd gone where pillared skies abound
for falling stars, tails winking bright,
but on a quiet street I found
a galaxy of Christmas lights.

Rachel Wallace-Oberle

MAGIC IN THE AIR

THERE'S magic in the air tonight,
All is still and stars are bright,
Frost crystals glisten in the lane,
And round the misty windowpane.

Village church bells start to ring,
Peace abounds in everything,
Trees are resting, branches bare,
Expectancy is everywhere.

When their nightly prayers are said,
Children snuggle down in bed,
Hopes and dreams all interweave,
Because tonight is Christmas Eve!

Brian H. Gent

COBWEBS

IT'S as if a factory process
Has been in place,
Mass-producing delicate,
Viscous fibres,
Turning the threads
Into tiny hammocks,
To be exported
To hang
On the frosty hedgerows
At dawn;
Here the money spiders
Ply their trade,
Seeking income
From passers-by
Who stop, pause — rest
Even for a millisecond.

David Elder

The artists are:-

Matt Bain; Winter Spirit, September.
Sheila Carmichael; Springtime Stakes.
Jackie Cartwright; Lark Or Owl?,
Magic In The Air.
Henri Damoiseaux; The Fountain.
Miranda Dear; A Charming Place.
John Dugan; The Old Covered Bridge,
The Fairy, Unhurried, Fireworks,
Christmas Lights.
Alan Haldane; Autumn Leaves.
Eunice Harvey; A Magic Night, Buddleia,
Summer's Ending.
Harry McGregor; Wild Garlic,
Fragments – Maytime, By The River.
Ian McIntosh; The Tranquil Hour,
Seasonal Views, Heron, Swifts.
Norma Maclean; Spring Morning,
Swallows, Encroachment,
Nocturnal Interplay, Among Trees.
Sandy Milligan; Geese, The Sinner,
Two Goldfinches, I Remember,
Polney Loch.
Keith Robson; Rumbling Bridge,
Dolgoch Falls, Branch-Line Train,
The Dreaming Place, Night,
Chestnut Traces, Rain, Storm.
Ruth M. L. Walker; Night-Imagery,
Dark Shadows.
Joseph Watson; When…
Staff Artists; Not Wasted Time, Fairies,
Umbrellas, To Jane, The Ruin,
Lines Composed In A Wood On A Windy
Day, The Mountain, Cobwebs.

JULY

S	1	8	15	22	29
M	2	9	16	23	30
Tu	3	10	17	24	31
W	4	11	18	25	—
Th	5	12	19	26	—
F	6	13	20	27	—
S	7	14	21	28	—

AUGUST

S	—	5	12	19	26
M	—	6	13	20	27
Tu	—	7	14	21	28
W	1	8	15	22	29
Th	2	9	16	23	30
F	3	10	17	24	31
S	4	11	18	25	—

SEPTEMBER

S		2	9	16	23	30
M		3	10	17	24	—
Tu		4	11	18	25	—
W		5	12	19	26	—
Th		6	13	20	27	—
F		7	14	21	28	—
S	1	8	15	22	29	—